I'm not *waiting* anymore

Letting go and
living your best life

Simran Bhandari

ISBN 978-93-343-7335-6

Dear Reader,

I love you.
And I hope you love yourself enough to stop waiting
for people who only meet you halfway.

Your heart was never too much.
It was never meant to beg for what it freely gave.
It was made to be held gently,
not used as a place for others to rest and leave.

I hope this book feels like a quiet hug.
A little reminder that soft is not weak.
That you don't have to become colder
just to feel safer.

This is for the ones who feel everything deeply.
Who stayed too long.
Who loved too hard.
Who are learning, slowly, to choose themselves again.

You're right.
I wrote this for you.

With love,
Simran Bhandari

Table of Contents

PART I: THE BREAKING

"Where it started hurting. Where we stayed too long. Where we lost ourselves."

I Just Wanted to Be Chosen

I didn't ask for forever,
just to be seen
on your good days,
not only when you were lonely.

I showed up,
even when it hurt.
Loved you through silences.
Waited,
even when I knew
you wouldn't stay.

You made me feel
like a guest
in a home I was building.

And still,
I stayed.

Not because you earned that love,
but because I didn't know
I deserved it too.

You reached for me only when it was convenient.
And that's what broke me,

not the leaving,
but how you stayed
without holding me close.

Now I know,
love shouldn't feel like
a question mark.

I wanted to be home.
You wanted shelter.
So you left
when the sky cleared.

And me?
I finally choose the calm.
I choose the healing.
I choose me.

I Was Loud Before Love

I laughed loud.
Spoke without shrinking.
Wore red on quiet days
just to feel alive.

I danced without waiting.
Felt everything fully.
Dreamed out loud.

Then love asked me to whisper.
And I did.
I tucked away my sparkle
so I'd be easier to hold.

But in shrinking,
I lost my sound.
Forgot my fire.

Now she's stirring,
the girl who glowed.
She's not asking this time.

She's just being,
loud,
soft,
fearlessly bright.

They Loved Me Like a Habit, Not a Heart

You didn't love me.
You just got used to me,
like background music,
always playing,
never truly heard.

I was your comfort,
not your choice.
You liked knowing I'd stay,
even when you didn't.

You came back
when the world felt heavy,
but never when your heart did.

And I called it love,
because I didn't know
what else to name
the feeling of being reached for
only in silence.

I was always there.
Maybe that's why you never feared losing me.

You liked me within reach,
but not within heart.

But I'm not a habit.
I'm a heart.
And I deserve to be loved
like one.

The Fear of Being Soft

I wasn't always guarded.
I used to feel out loud.
Cry freely.
Say "I miss you" first.

But softness got me hurt.
Kindness got misunderstood.
So I hid,
behind smiles,
behind "I'm fine."

Because tenderness became a target.

But now,
healing reminds me,
maybe the fear
was never mine.
Maybe others just didn't know
how to hold gentle things.

So I'm learning,
to feel again.
To speak when it aches.
To cry without shame.

Softness is what stayed

when nothing else did.

And I,
I'm ready to feel again.

Lonely Next to You

You were right next to me,
and I still felt alone.
Isn't that the worst kind of loneliness?
When someone's body stays,
but their heart has already gone?

I used to think love meant presence.
But you were there,
just not with me.
Not really.

I told you quiet truths,
hoping you'd hear me.
But you only nodded,
like my feelings were noise.

I cried some nights
with my back turned,
not because you hurt me on purpose,
but because you didn't even notice.

You thought being there was enough.
But a shadow is not love.
A heartbeat isn't a hug.

I reached for you,

again and again.
But you were always
just one step too far.

And now,
I'm done reaching.

I deserve more
than feeling invisible
in someone else's arms.

You were beside me.
But my heart
was never lonelier.

I Was in Love With Someone Who Wasn't Real

Maybe the hardest part
is knowing I wasn't in love with you,
but with the version I made up.

The one who held my hand like it meant something.
Who spoke to me like I was rare.
The one who promised softness
and made it feel real.

But it wasn't.
You changed.
Or maybe you were never that person to begin with
and I just didn't want to see it.

I kept waiting,
thinking you'd come back
to who you were at the start.

But,
that version of you
never truly existed.

You were an echo,
a dream I didn't want to let go.

And I waited at a door you stopped knocking on.

But how do you return
to a place you never lived?

Now,
I'm learning to let go,
of someone
who was never really here.

The Day I Knew You'd Never Choose Me

There was no big moment.
No loud goodbye.
Just a quiet ache
that told me,
you were never building anything that had space for me.

Not fully.
Not the way I kept choosing you.
Not the way I needed.

You liked me, maybe.
But love?
Love shows up.
And you never did.

I curled up in the doorway of your silence.
For effort that never arrived.
For you to notice
how tired I was of pretending I was okay.

But you didn't.

And one day,
with a heavy heart and swollen eyes,
I finally said,
this isn't love.

This is waiting.

And I deserve more
than being someone's maybe.

So I let go.
Not because I stopped loving you,
but because I finally
started loving me.

I Blamed Myself When You Hurt Me

You didn't need to yell.
A sigh,
a cold look,
was enough to make me feel like I did something wrong.

And I believed it.
Every time.
Maybe I said too much.
Maybe I asked for too much.
Maybe it was me.

You never said sorry.
Never held space for my hurt.
You made my feelings feel like noise.
Like I was overflowing,
too tender to touch,
too real to hold.

So I turned it inward.
I shrank.
I softened my voice.
I blamed my heart for wanting more.

But no matter how small I became,
you kept hurting me,
quietly.

That's the thing about toxic love.
It doesn't always shout.
It just makes you doubt yourself
until you forget what love is supposed to feel like.

But not anymore.

Now, I speak when it hurts.
Now, I protect my peace.
Because love should never
make you bleed
and then blame you for the wound.

You Promised Forever, But Meant Until It Got Hard

You said forever
like it was real.
Like it meant something.
But your love only stayed
while things were easy.

You adored the petals,
feared the thorns,
the smiles,
the calm,
the comfort.

But love isn't just soft mornings.
It's staying
when it's messy.
It's choosing someone,
even when it's hard.

And you,
You slipped out like Sunday evening.

You called my depth "too much,"
my care "too clingy,"
my heart "too heavy."

I tried to bring us back
to the beginning,
but you had already let go.

You promised forever,
but your forever ended
the moment I needed more
than just your presence.

So no,
I won't romanticize it anymore.

Forever isn't a pretty word,
it's a choice.
One you never made.

And now,
I miss who I was
before I believed you.

Love Was a Game

Welcome back to
"Love Me or Leave Me"
where the rules kept changing
and the prize was pain.

Say nothing.
Need nothing.
Smile anyway.
Lose points if you cry.

You were the host,
the judge,
the crowd.
And I?
Just the one performing
for love.

Each day a test,
too much?
too little?
never quite right.

Still,
I played.
Changed.
Shrank.

But I'm out of pieces now.
Out of roles to play.

And..
I'm done.

Because real love
isn't a show.
And I'm not
a contestant.

I Thought Loyalty Would Be Enough

I stayed.
Even when it hurt.
Even when my heart whispered,
"This isn't love."

I defended you.
Chose you.
Hoped you'd see my worth
because I never walked away.

I thought being loyal
would make you stay too.

But loyalty can't fix
what someone won't hold.
It can't grow flowers
in a place that was never soil.

You took my loyalty for weakness,
loved me halfway,
because you knew I wouldn't leave.

But enduring emptiness
doesn't make it devotion.
It's losing yourself slowly,
while calling it devotion.

And I've done enough of that.

So now,
I choose a different kind of loyalty,
the kind that starts with me.

I was always loyal.
But now,
I'm loyal to my peace.

Pain Doesn't Need Permission

You rolled your eyes
when I cried.
Called me "too much"
for feeling deeply.

But pain doesn't wait
for permission.
It doesn't shrink
just because you do.

You heard the thunder,
never saw the damage.

I tried to explain.
Then I stopped.
And still,
you didn't ask what hurt.

But I don't need
my pain to be quiet
for it to be real.

It was.
Even if you didn't stay
long enough to see it.

I won’t soften it
to make it easier for you.

Because pain,
like love,
exists,
without your permission.

The Pain of Almost

We were never fully real,
were we?
Not a love story,
just an almost.

A love unfinished.
A door half-open.

But almost hurts in its own way,
because there was nothing to end,
just a feeling left open.

I remember the looks,
the near-promises,
the way you held my hand
when it was easy
and let go
when it asked for more.

I thought you were scared.
I thought if I stayed patient,
you'd stay too.

But you never promised anything,
and I kept hoping anyway.

You liked the version of me
who didn't need answers.
Who smiled through the guessing.

And I...
I wanted you to choose me.
Fully. Finally.
But you never did.

Now I know,
I deserve a love
that doesn't leave me unsure.

We weren't a tragedy.
We were a quiet ache.
The kind that lingers
every time I think
about what we never became.

You Never Said Sorry

You never said sorry.
Not even when you saw the hurt
in my quiet eyes.
You just said,
"It wasn't that deep."

But it was.
To me.

It was deep
when I stayed up overthinking.
When I smiled at your name
even after all the hurt.
When I defended you
while you stayed silent.

I loved you
in ways you never saw.
And you left
like none of it mattered.

Maybe it didn't.
But don't ever tell someone
their ocean was just a puddle
because you never dove in.

You didn't need to love me back.
But you could've said,
"You mattered."

Instead,
you shrugged.
Left me holding words
you never had the courage to speak.

Now I know,
silence isn't peace.
And love,
even unreturned,
still deserves to be honored.

I Left Quietly

You thought I'd stay,
no matter how often you forgot to show up.
You mistook my softness for weakness,
my silence for yes,
my love for something you'd always have.

But I wasn't staying
because I couldn't leave.
I stayed
because I believed in us.
In growth. In change.

But every time I gave more,
you gave less.
And still,
I tried harder.
Hoping you'd notice.
Hoping you'd care.

I bent so much,
I lost pieces of myself.
You gave me just enough
to keep me hoping,
never enough to make me feel whole.

You thought I'd stay forever.

Because leaving felt louder than love.

But soft doesn't mean blind.
And love,
real love,
shouldn't hurt this much to hold.

So one day,
quietly,
I left.

Not because I stopped loving you.
But because I finally
started loving me.

PART II: THE GRIEVING

"The silence after goodbye. The ache of missing someone.
The war between holding on and letting go."

I Still Dream of You

You still visit me in my dreams.
And there,
you're gentle again.
You laugh like before,
look at me like I still matter.

No distance.
No silence.
Just us,
the way we were.

I wake with an ache
I thought I buried.
Your name still lingers
in quiet corners of my mind.

Some nights,
I wish the dream was real.
That you'd call.
That you'd say
you never stopped loving me.

But I know better.
Dreams lie.
They show us
what we still long for.

And when the world sleeps,
my heart forgets you're gone.

When Healing Hurts

No one tells you
that healing hurts.

It's not a clean break,
it's slow.
A thousand little goodbyes
to memories you swore you'd keep.

I thought healing would feel like peace.
But some days,
it feels like emptiness.
Like silence where your voice once lived.

Some days, I'm okay.
I smile.
I breathe.
And then,
a song, a scent,
a street we walked,
and I'm breaking again.

That's grief.
It doesn't ask.
It just returns,
softly, suddenly.

And I let it.

Because healing
isn't perfect.
It's choosing yourself
again and again,
even when part of you
still misses them.

No, I'm not there yet.
But I'm trying.
And for now,
that's enough.

I Hope You Remember Me Softly

I don't want to be a ghost
you try to forget.
Or a name
that tightens your chest.

I hope you remember
how I loved,
how I stayed,
how I tried,
even when it hurt.

Remember the small things,
the softness,
the way I listened
even when I wasn't heard.

I hope you remember my laugh,
not just the tears.
The way I looked at you
like you were everything.

You couldn't love me
the way I needed.
And maybe,
you never could.

But I don't hate you.

You gave me something,
even if it wasn't forever.
And it taught me
what love should feel like,
and what it shouldn't.

So if you ever think of me,
let it be with peace.
With gratitude.
With the quiet truth
that I loved you
fully.

And that,
for a moment,
you were chosen.

Some Nights Still Hurt

I wish I could say it's easy.
That time has softened it all.
But some nights,
they still hurt
more than others.

It comes quietly.
Your name in a song.
A laugh that sounds like yours.
A memory I didn't invite.

I still pause
before ordering your coffee.
Still scroll through old messages
I meant to delete.

Grief isn't always loud.
Sometimes it's just
feeling empty
in a room full of people.
Smiling,
while your chest quietly aches.

I cracked where the light tried to get in.
I'm healing,
but healing doesn't mean

I don't miss you.
It just means
I'm learning how to carry it.

So tonight,
if it feels heavy,
I won't run.
I'll sit with it.

Because even this pain
reminds me,
it was real.

I Still Catch Myself Waiting

I don't wait for your calls.
I've let go
of the little ways I used to hold on.

But still
I catch myself waiting.

In the way I pause
before sharing good news,
like I'm about to tell you.
In the way my heart flinches
at a voice that sounds like yours.

I know you're gone.
But grief moves slow.
And mine still beats
in your name sometimes.

I don't want you back.
I just miss being loved,
even halfway.

Maybe I'm not waiting for you.
Maybe just the version
I once believed you could be.

But today,
I remind myself,
I'm not waiting anymore.

I Wasn't Allowed to Break

You were allowed to pull away,
to go quiet,
to vanish for days,
and I'd still be the one reaching out.

But the moment I needed something,
you disappeared.

I wasn't allowed to hurt.
You saw me as the strong one,
the one who always came back,
even while breaking.

It's exhausting
to carry everything,
to hold space for two
in a love built on silence.

I needed you to stay
when I was falling apart.
To say,
"I've got you."
But you never did.

I kept picking up my own pieces
while holding yours too.

And I called that love.

But it wasn't.
It was loneliness
disguised as loyalty.

I should've been allowed
to fall apart,
to be held,
just once.

But you only loved me
when I was easy.

And I'm done
being strong for both of us.

I Didn’t Know How to Let You Go

Letting go wasn’t just leaving.
It was staying in the past
long after you were gone.
Still hearing your name
in songs.
Still saving space
you no longer filled.

It wasn’t loud.
It was quiet.
Like deleting your number
but still remembering it.
Like clearing your photos
but not the memories.

I kept asking,
how do you let go
of someone
who felt like home?

But the truth is,
you let go first.
And I was holding on
to something already gone.

You didn’t just leave,

you took parts of me with you.
The part that believed
love was enough.

Now I'm grieving
someone who's still alive.
Still out there.
Just not mine.

And that grief
has no goodbye.
Just silence.

But I'm learning
slowly
to let go of you
without losing me.

I Miss Who I Was With You

I don’t just miss you—
I miss who I was
when I thought you loved me.

Back then,
I smiled easier.
Loved louder.
Ignored red flags
just to feel chosen.

I gave so much
I didn’t notice
how empty I was becoming.

Now that you're gone,
I miss the version of me
who still believed.
Who folded herself in love that didn’t fit.
Who kept dreaming.

And some days,
I grieve her too.

But now,
something stronger is growing.
And maybe one day,

I'll love who I'm becoming
even more
than who I was
when I loved you.

The Illusion of Love

I thought I missed you.
But really,
I missed the version
I made up.

You weren't soft.
You weren't there.
But I painted over the cracks
and called it love.

I memorized what wasn't real
To the hope of who you could be,
not who you were.

You were silence.
I called it mystery.
You were distant.
I called it deep.

I didn't love you.
I loved being wanted.
Even if it wasn't real.

Funny,
how we break our hearts
over people

who were never even trying.

So no,
I don't miss you.
I miss the story
I told myself.

Now,
I'm done with pretending.
And this time,
I'm choosing love that's real.

I Wanted You to Hurt Too

I said I was healing.
Said I forgave you.
But in the quiet,
I still wanted it to hurt you,
just once.
Just enough to know
I mattered.

I wanted a song
to break you like it broke me.
A memory
to catch you off guard.

Not out of hate,
but because I loved you,
and you let go
like it was easy.

While I stayed up
begging the stars,
you slept like peace.

I wanted it to sting.
Just enough to feel
like I wasn't the only one aching.

But now I know,
your pain
won't fix mine.

And healing
isn't about whether you feel sorry.

So maybe you'll feel it.
Maybe you won't.

But I'm done
waiting for your ache.

I have softer things
to hope for now.

I Don't Cry for You Anymore

I don't cry for you
like I used to.
Not in the dark,
not in the silence.

But still
I break
in quieter ways.

Like when I laugh
and forget you're not there to share it.
Or when a song plays
and your memory hums along.

I smile when people ask,
like it doesn't ache.
Like I'm okay.

Maybe I've healed,
a little.
But healing isn't forgetting.
And silence
doesn't always mean peace.

Sometimes I still think
of the version of us

that almost was.

Sometimes I wonder
if you think of me too,
just for a moment.

I don't want you back.
But I do want
to stop breaking in places
no one sees.

Because even without tears,
some parts of me
still whisper your name.

I Thought I Was Over You

It played softly,
a song we used to hum
without thinking.
And suddenly,
I was back in your car,
windows down,
your smile stealing glances
I still remember.

Funny how songs hold memories.

I thought I'd moved on.
Maybe I had.
But healing is quiet,
and sometimes it echoes
in the most ordinary things.

It wasn't the song's fault,
it just brought you back,
for a moment.

And I let it.

Let myself miss you,
just for a beat,
before placing the feeling

back where I don't reach anymore.

Because missing you
doesn't mean I want you back.
It just means
what we had was real.

So I let the song play.
Didn't skip.
Didn't cry.

Just listened,
with a heart that flinched,
but didn't break.

And that,
I think,
is healing too.

You Let Me Leave

I didn't need big gestures.
Just for you to stop me.
To say,
"Wait. Don't go."

You watched me walk away like
I was a Sunday you barely remembered.
like I was just a page,
not your favorite chapter.

That's what hurt,
not the goodbye,
but the silence.
The way you didn't try.

I waited.
Made excuses.
Hoped you'd reach out.
You never did.

And slowly,
I stopped waiting.
Not because I stopped caring,
but because I saw the truth:

If someone can let you go

without a fight,
they were never really holding on.

So I let go, too.
Not with anger.
Just quiet grief,
for being the only one
who ever stayed.

You Left, But the Questions Stayed

You're gone,
but the questions stayed.

Did you love me,
or was I just there
when you felt alone?

Were your words real,
or just comfort
in passing moments?

I know I won't get answers.
Not at 2 a.m.,
when your silence feels loudest.

Maybe closure
is something we build
from what's left behind.

But still,
the questions come.
Quiet. Sharp.
Unanswered.

I reread your messages,
the ones that felt half-hearted.

I wonder,
did you know it hurt?
Or did you just not care?

And then I feel foolish,
for needing clarity
from someone
who never gave it.

But that's grief.
It shows up without warning,
wearing your name,
asking things
you never stayed long enough to answer.

My Heart Learns Slowly

My mind knows you're gone.
It remembers the silence,
the waiting,
the way I bent to be loved.

It's moved on.
Let go.
Closed the door.

But my heart?
She's still catching up.
Still searching the quiet
for your name.
Still stumbling
when she hears your song.

It's strange
to know better,
but still ache.

I don't want you back.
I just miss
what I hoped you'd be.
I miss the me
who still believed.

But maybe that's okay.

Grief doesn't follow rules.
And healing
takes time.

So I won't rush her.
She's soft.
She's slow.
But she's learning.

And one day,
she'll let go too.

PART III: THE REMEMBERING

"The moment you realize: maybe I didn't deserve that. Maybe I was never the problem."

It Wasn't Love

I kept calling it love,
even when it hurt,
even when I begged
for crumbs of care.

But it wasn't love.
It was loneliness
in disguise,
wrapped in sweet words
and half-hearted hugs.

Real love doesn't
make you feel small.
It doesn't punish your softness
or make you question your worth.

What we had
wasn't connection.
It was need.
You stayed to fill your silence.
I stayed to avoid mine.

But I know now,
being alone
isn't the same
as being unloved.

You didn't love me.
You just didn't want to be alone.
And I...
I hadn't learned
how to choose myself yet.

But I have now.
And that truth
sets me free.

Soft Isn't Weak

I used to think
my softness made them leave.
That if I was colder,
quieter,
less,
they would've stayed.

But now I know,
Being soft after heartbreak is the real rebellion.

It takes strength
to keep loving
after being hurt.
To feel deeply
and still choose kindness.

You mistook my depth for chaos.
Too emotional.
Too sensitive.
But you just weren't ready
for a love this full.

And that's not on me.

I won't apologize
for my open heart,

for crying at beauty,
for loving out loud.

My softness is not a flaw,
it's a home.
And one day,
someone will walk in
and never want to leave.

Because this softness?
It was never the problem.

Dear Me, I'm Sorry

I'm sorry
for not protecting you.
For calling you "too much"
when you were just honest.
For choosing them
over you,
again and again.

You wanted love.
You stayed soft.
Even when I blamed you
for being left.

But not anymore.

Now,
I'm listening.
I'm staying.
I'm holding you
the way I always wished
someone else would.

This isn't just sorry,
it's a promise.

I promise to put you first.

To stop giving your heart
to those who never earned it.
To love you
like you always deserved.

You've always been enough.
And this time,
I'm not leaving you.

You Didn't Break Me

For a long time,
I blamed you,
thought you ruined me,
made me feel
too much,
too needy.

But,
you didn't break me.
You just showed me
where I was already hurting.

You reminded me
of wounds I never healed,
of the lie
that I had to earn love
to be enough.

You weren't the first to leave.
But you left in a way
that made me finally see
how long I'd been
leaving myself.

And for that,
I don't hate you.

I thank you.

Because now,
I give myself the love
I once begged for.
Now,
I choose me.

You were the lesson,
not the loss.

So no,
you didn't break me.
You woke me up.

And now,
I'm whole.

If You Met Me Now

If you met me now,
you wouldn't know what to do.

I speak up.
I ask for what I need.
I don't shrink
to fit small love.

You once called me "too much."
But now I know,
you just weren't enough.

You couldn't hold
a woman who no longer bends.
No more waiting.
No more half-love.
No more doors left open
for those who leave.

This version of me?
She glows without guilt.
She chooses herself, fully.

And you?
You never stayed long enough
to see her rise.

I'm Not Bitter, Just Honest

I used to defend you,
to others,
to myself,
to the truth.

I said you were scared.
Confused.
Not trying to hurt me.

But,
you knew.
You knew I was all in
while you stayed halfway.
You saw my open heart
and still walked away.

I'm not bitter.
I'm just done pretending
you didn't choose to let me down.

You weren't confused,
you were careless.
You weren't lost,
you just didn't choose me.

And I kept turning red flags

into something softer
just to hold on.

But now,
I see clearly.
And that's not bitterness,
that's freedom.

You weren't the one.
Not because I wasn't enough,
but because you weren't ready
for love this deep.

So no,
I'm not bitter.
I'm just finally telling the truth.

Convenience Isn't Love

Don't say I was complicated.
I just asked for consistency.

Don't call me demanding.
I just refused to settle for scraps.

You didn't love me deeply
because that would've required effort
and you?
You mistook comfort for commitment.

You didn't need someone easy.
You needed someone who would shrink.
And I didn't.

So no,
I wasn't hard to love.
You were just lazy.
And I finally got tired
of lowering the bar

I Wasn't Hard to Love

For a long time,
I thought it was me.
Full of feeling.
Full of fire.
Not built for shallow hands.

But the truth is,
I wasn't hard to love.
You just didn't know how.

You didn't know how to stay,
how to listen,
how to love someone
who felt deeply
and asked gently.

I made excuses.
Told myself love
was supposed to be hard.
But real love
doesn't make you beg.
Doesn't make you question your worth.

I wasn't too much.
I was just too real
for someone

who wasn't ready.

That's not my burden anymore.

The right person
won't run from my softness.
They'll see it,
and stay.

Because I finally know:
their limits
were never a mirror
of my value.

I Stayed Because I Was Afraid to Start Over

I didn't stay
because I was happy.
I stayed
because letting go
meant facing the truth.

I held on,
not to love,
but to comfort.
To routine.
To the hope
that maybe things would change.

Sometimes hurt becomes home
because it's known.

I told myself,
"Just wait a little longer."
But waiting
only taught me
how to live with less.

Now I know,
starting over isn't what breaks you.

Staying in what hurts
does.

Letting go
wasn't leaving you.
It was choosing me.
Choosing peace
over patterns.
Freedom
over fear.

And though I still grieve
what we never became,
I'm proud of the me
who finally walked away.

The Day I Found Me

At first,
I thought I lost something rare.
You felt like home,
even when it burned.

So I grieved.
Like I lost everything.

But with time,
I saw the truth.

I didn't lose you.
I lost the illusion.
The dream of who I hoped you were.

What I found
was me.

The me who stopped begging.
Stopped explaining.
Started listening,
to her own heart.

I found peace
in the quiet you left behind.
I found my voice

in the silence.

You weren't my ending,
you were the mirror.

You showed me
where I still needed healing.
Where I still needed
to believe I was enough.

Now, I do.

So no,
I don't regret you.
But I won't return.

Because what I've found now
is real.
It's mine.
It's me.

I Don’t Need You to Understand

There was a time
I wanted you to see
how much I loved you,
how much it hurt
to be close,
yet never chosen.

I waited for you
to realize what you lost.
To say, “I’m sorry.”

But I’ve let that go.

Because needing your understanding
kept me tied
to a hope
that never came.

Closure isn’t always a conversation.
Sometimes,
it’s a quiet choice,
to stop waiting,
to stop needing.

You don’t have to see it now.
You don’t have to say a word.

Because I see it.
I know I deserved more.
And that's enough.

I lived it.
I felt it.
I healed.

So no,
I don't need you to understand.

I do.
And that's all I need
to be free.

I Finally Chose Me

I used to think
choosing me
meant losing you.
That walking away
was giving up.

But I was wrong.
Choosing me
was the beginning,
of peace,
of calm mornings,
of no longer proving
I'm enough.

You taught me something,
not by staying,
but by leaving.
By loving me in pieces
I tried to make whole.

But I was never broken.
I just gave too much
to someone
who gave too little.

Choosing me

meant letting go
of the girl who thought
love meant sacrifice.

It meant finding peace
in my own company,
more than I ever found
next to you.

I chose me.
Not to prove anything,
but because my heart
deserves to feel safe.

And now I know,
the one who'll protect it best
is me.

Love Isn't a Performance

I used to treat love
like a stage.
Always adjusting,
always asking,
"Am I enough like this?"

I watched your silence
like lines to learn.
Smiled on cue.
Held back tears.
Became quieter,
just to keep you close.

But even then,
you left.

Because real love
doesn't need rehearsals.
It needs truth.
It needs presence.

I'm done playing roles
just to be loved.
Done shrinking.

I want a love

where I can breathe.
Where I don't need to perform
to be kept.

Love isn't a show.
And I'm done acting
like I'm not enough.

I Know What I Bring

I used to beg
to be chosen.
To be enough
for someone
who never even showed up
for the love I offered.

I gave everything,
softness, loyalty, care,
and blamed myself
when it wasn't returned.

But not anymore.

Now I know
what I bring.
My love is rare.
My presence is real.
I give fully,
feel deeply,
and stay true.

I don't play games.
I don't hide my heart.
I don't run.

I bring honesty.
I bring warmth.
I bring a light
that won't be dimmed.

And from now on,
I won't beg.
I won't shrink.
I won't shrink into invisible spaces anymore.

If you can't meet me with grace,
you don't get a seat.

Because I'm not too much.
I'm something beautiful.
And only those who see that
will get the chance
to hold it.

I'm Not Waiting Anymore

I used to wait,
for your message,
your apology,
your change of heart.

I waited through holidays,
quiet moments,
days I wished you were still here.

But I'm not waiting anymore.

Because waiting
for someone who won't show up
isn't love,
it's losing yourself
piece by piece.

I made excuses.
Held on to maybes.
Softened my voice
just to feel seen.

But love
doesn't keep you silent.
It doesn't ask you
to stay small and still.

Now,
I choose forward.
I choose me.

You may cross my mind,
but you no longer hold it still.

I won't hold my breath
for someone
who never breathed beside me.

So no,
I'm not waiting anymore.
Not for answers.
Not for you.

I've already chosen
what you didn't.

I Forgive Myself

I used to feel guilty
for not walking away sooner.
For ignoring the signs.
For hoping
when I should've let go.

I stayed,
even when it hurt.
Even when you stopped trying.
And for a while,
I blamed myself.

But now I know,
I stayed
because I loved deeply.
Because I believed
people could change.

That kind of heart
isn't weakness.
It's courage.

There's no shame
in hoping,
in being loyal,
in giving someone a chance.

What matters is,
I finally chose me.
I listened to the voice
that said,
"You don't have to keep breaking."

So today,
I forgive myself,
for staying too long,
for loving too hard,
for not knowing better
until I did.

And that,
is enough.

PART IV: THE RETURNING

"Coming back to yourself. Coming back home. Choosing softness and strength again."

The Day I Chose Me

There was no big goodbye.
No drama.
Just a quiet moment,
me in the mirror,
whispering,
"I can't keep doing this."

I had given love,
forgiveness,
hope,
and lost pieces of myself in return.

One day,
I just got tired.
Tired of waiting.
Tired of hurting.
Tired of mistaking pain
for love.

So I stopped hoping you'd choose me.
And I chose myself.

It didn't feel loud.
It felt like peace.
Like finally breathing.

I asked,
"What do I need?"
And I listened.

No one clapped.
But I did.
Inside.

Because that was the day
I stopped surviving for you,
and started living
for me.

I Am My Own Safe Place

I used to look for safety
in someone else,
in their arms,
their words,
their love.

I thought being chosen
would finally bring peace.

But now I know,
real safety
comes from within.

I am my own safe place now.
The calm after the storm.
The soft voice that says,
"It's okay. You're safe with me."

I don't wait for rescue anymore.
I've built a home
inside myself,
steady,
soft,
enough.

Some days still ache.

Some nights still sting.
But even in the quiet,
I am held.

By me.

And that,
no one can take away.

I'm Not Who I Was

I don't say it with anger,
I say it with peace.

The girl who loved you
was gentle,
hopeful,
willing to shrink
just to be held.

She stayed quiet.
She stayed soft.
She stayed until she disappeared.

But she's not here anymore.

Not because she failed,
but because she grew.

Now, I speak.
I ask.
I walk away
from almost-love
and half-hearted effort.

I still love deeply,
but with boundaries now.

With truth.
With strength.

So no,
I'm not who I was
when I loved you.

And I'm proud of that.
Because healing didn't just bring me back,
it brought me home
to someone stronger.

To me.

Becoming Light Again

I used to carry everything,
unspoken words,
unmet love,
the ache of not being enough.

I moved through life
heavy,
guarded,
tired.

But healing came softly.
And I started letting go,
one memory,
one apology,
one old version of me.

And slowly,
I felt light again.

Not because I forgot,
but because I stopped
holding what no longer belonged to me.

I laughed without guilt.
Breathed without pain.
Saw beauty again

in sunlight,
in music,
in peace.

That's healing,
quiet and slow,
until one day
you realize
you're floating.

I am becoming light again.
And this time,
no one gets to dim it.

I'm Proud I Stayed Soft

They could've made me hard,
the leaving,
the lies,
the silence.

There were so many chances
to close my heart,
to stop feeling.

But I didn't.
And I'm proud of that.

I stayed soft
in a world
that called it weakness.
I kept loving,
kept hoping,
kept being kind.

I was hurt,
but I didn't hurt others.
I was broken,
but I never broke anyone back.

There is strength
in choosing softness,

in healing without hate,
in feeling deeply
and still believing in love.

So no,
I'm not ashamed
of my heart.
Of how much I care.
Of how soft I still am.

Because this softness
isn't my flaw.
It's my power.
It's my truth.

And no one
can take that from me.

Coming Home to Me

For so long,
I searched for home
in others,
in their arms,
their words,
their warmth.

But home isn't them.
It's me.
It always was.

It's in how I hold myself
when no one else does.
How I breathe,
how I laugh,
how I stay soft
even in silence.

Coming home
meant unlearning the need
for outside love
to feel whole.

It meant knowing
I am enough,
as I am.

That my own arms
are safe.
That my soul
is worth returning to.

No noise.
No rush.
Just a soft knowing.

I was never lost.
Just waiting
to come back
to me.

I Am Still Capable of Beautiful Things

Some days,
I forgot.
The heartbreak felt too heavy
to hold hope.

But still,
I stayed.
I whispered light
into the dark.

And now,
I feel it.
A gentle return
to joy.
To peace.
To me.

I smile without guilt.
I breathe without ache.
I find beauty again,
in sunlight,
in music,
in stillness.

I am still capable
of beautiful things.

Of soft beginnings.
Of love
that starts within.

This chapter
isn't about who left.
It's about who I'm becoming.

I am not my pain.
I am how I rose from it.

And today,
I believe again,
in beautiful things,
especially
the ones I plant myself.

To the One I'm Becoming

I see you now,
not the girl who begged,
not the heart that broke in silence,
but the woman rising.

Soft,
but no longer sorry.
Hopeful,
but no longer waiting.

You move with calm now.
Breathe steady.
Stand whole.

You're still healing,
still learning,
but you're showing up,
every day.

And I'm proud.
Proud of how you chose yourself.
How you stayed soft
in a world that wanted you cold.

To the one I'm becoming,
thank you.

For not giving up.
For growing into someone
I now call home.

You are not what hurt you.
You are what healed.

I Don't Need Saving

I used to wait
for someone to fix it,
to love the pain away,
to hold me
until I forgot the hurt.

I wanted rescue.
From the ache,
the memories,
the weight.

But I've stopped waiting.
No one's coming.
And that's okay.
Because now,
I don't need saving.

I've learned
to hold myself
on the hard nights,
to breathe through the pain,
to find peace
where grief once lived.

I still long for love,
but not to feel whole.

Just to walk beside me.

Because I am already standing.
Already enough.
Already home.

The girl who once begged for rescue
became the woman
who saved herself.

I'm at Peace with the Past

There was a time
I replayed it all,
the words,
the silence,
the chances I shouldn't have given.

I carried it
like a weight,
like a wound.

But now,
when memories come,
I don't flinch.

I see them as they were,
lessons,
not life sentences.

It hurt.
But it shaped me.
It taught me what I deserve.

And now,
I choose peace.
Gently.
Fully.

Every day.

The past no longer decides
who I am
or how I love.

I made it through.
And when I look back,
I don't feel pain.

I feel gratitude.
Because it led me
back home
to me.

To the One Who Comes After

I'm not asking you to fix
what someone else broke.

I'm not expecting you to heal
wounds that were never yours.

But if you stay,
stay gently.

I'm no longer performing
to be chosen.
I no longer bend
to keep someone interested.

I've learned to stand on my own,
but if you reach for me,
I'll reach back,
only if it feels safe to open again.

Come softly.
And meet me where I already am:
whole,
but still human.

There's Still So Much Ahead

For a while,
everything felt dull.
The days blurred.
Joy faded.
Life felt far away.

But healing is slow.
And one day,
the sun felt warm again.
The coffee tasted soft.
The silence felt like peace.

And I knew,
there's still so much
to look forward to.

New mornings.
Safe love.
Laughter without fear.
Words that feel like home.

There are books to read,
places to see,
people I haven't met
who will see me clearly.

Life isn't behind me.
It's here.
It's coming.

And for the first time in a while,
I believe in it again.

Learning to Trust Again

There was a time
I trusted nothing,
not love,
not people,
not even myself.

I moved through life
expecting the worst,
because it had come before.

I thought heartbreak made me wise,
but it just made me afraid.

Afraid to hope.
Afraid to believe.
Afraid to begin.

But slowly,
life is showing me
that not everything wants to hurt me.

Some things hold gently.
Some people stay.
Some days are soft
without warning.

I'm learning to trust again,
not blindly,
but bravely.

Trusting myself,
my feelings,
my voice.

Trusting that I can walk away
from anything
that forgets my worth.

Life isn't perfect,
but it still holds beauty.

And now,
I'm open to it again.

Love Will Come Again, But I'm Not Waiting

I used to wait for love,
like I had to earn it.
Like I had to be perfect
to be chosen.

I stayed in places
that didn't feel like love
and called it hope.

But now I know,
real love doesn't ask you
to shrink.
It stays
when you speak your truth.
It feels like peace,
not pressure.

And yes—
love will come again.
But I'm not waiting.

I won't pause my life
for someone
to see my worth.

I won't hold my breath
for hands
that never reach back.

I'm living.
I'm blooming.
I'm here.

And when love comes,
it won't save me.
It will join me—
in the life
I built on my own.

I'm Finally Home

Not in someone else.
Not in the past.
But here,
in me.

After the heartbreak,
the unraveling,
the ache I thought was love,
I've arrived.

It was slow.
Quiet.
A path of letting go
and coming back.

I no longer chase love
outside of me.
I no longer wait
to be chosen.

Because I am whole,
even with scars.
Even with stories
that still hum beneath the skin.

I've built peace

from pieces.
Planted softness
where pain once lived.

And now,
I stand in my light,
not to be seen,
but because it's mine.

This is healing.

Not perfect.
But present.
Not forgetting.
Just forgiving.

And after everything,
I'm home.

A Goodbye That Begins Again

This goodbye
doesn't shatter.
It doesn't beg or blame.
It simply lets go,
with soft eyes
and a steady heart.

I'm not just saying goodbye to you,
but to the version of me
who waited,
who clung,
who broke just to belong.

I'm releasing the silence,
the almosts,
the ache I called love.

And in this letting go,
I feel a beginning.

Not loud,
but peaceful,
like the first breath
after a storm.

This is where I stop waiting.

Where I choose me,
fully.

So if this is goodbye,
let it also be hello,
to healing,
to peace,
to the me
who was always coming home.

Dear You,

If you've made it to the end of this book, thank you, truly.. for carrying these words with you.

I didn't write this with the goal of creating a happy ending. I wrote it as a way back to myself, and maybe, in some way, a way back to you too.

Healing isn't linear. Some days you'll feel strong and sure, and some days it might still ache like it just happened. Both of those days are real, and both are okay.

This book isn't a guide. It's a mirror. And if even one poem helped you see yourself more clearly, or reminded you that your softness is still a strength, then that's more than enough.

You are not too much. You are not broken. You are not alone.

And I'm so glad you stayed.

With love,
Simran

www.ingramcontent.com/pod-product-compliance
Ingram Content Group UK Ltd.
Pitfield, Milton Keynes, MK11 3LW, UK
UKHW041314190726
13845UKWH00025B/262

9 789334 373356